POEMS OF THE VIETNAM WAR

Jocelyn Hollis

Philadelphia
AMERICAN POETRY AND LITERATURE PRESS

First Printing . . . . August 1980
Second Printing . . . . Sept. 1985
Revised Edition . . . . April 1987

Library of Congress Cataloging-in-Publication Data

Hollis, Jocelyn.
    Poems of the Vietnam War.

    Includes indexes.
    1. Vietnamese Conflict, 1961-1975—Poetry.
I. Title.
PS3558.03545P6   1987   811'.54   86-28776
ISBN 0-933486-67-7
ISBN 0-933486-68-5 (lib. bdg.)
ISBN 0-933486-69-3 (pbk.)

American Poetry and Literature Press, P.O. Box 2013, Upper Darby, PA. 19082. Trademark registered in U.S. Patent and Trademark Office

TABLE OF CONTENTS

BY A FATHER, TO HIS SON, DEAD ON THE BATTLEFIELD

Seed of my seed that lies
under the Asiatic snow
was it all wasted? Wise
men will not tell you so;
the wise have no way to know:
they have not gone where he lies,
my son of long ago
whose death was quick or slow
without my hand to seize
or touch his lips, or blow
my breath into his breath
in that last desperate try
that life will make at death
when all the balances go,
or kiss him, or let flow
a father's last fierce cries
torn from me like a blow
against the foolish law that says we take
the young before the old. Exchange,
O God, my tired soul for his young heart;
let me, that he may rise,
lie down in some far field
where all the false wars start.
For this cause, a man dies,
not for a statesman's lies,
but for the splendid reasons of the heart.

A MOTHER THINKS OF THE FATE OF CHILDREN

When I was born between the wars
that take our fathers and our sons
I looked around and saw the toys
my brothers loved, the little guns,

toy tanks, tin soldiers, grenadiers,
a knight, some castles, trucks, a rope;
all that man can invent of tears
and all that he can lose of hope.

Now they are grown, they have not gone
to war, no, nor their sons also.
But I, who need to love them, know
how war waits till the full crops grow
then drops them swiftly, row on row.

THE REGISTRAR AT THE DRAFT BOARD

Anyone who became eighteen
on that hot day in sixty-five
will have my name on his draft card
whether he's dead or alive.

Perhaps his parents keep it safe
locked with a silver cross or two,
some other metals, an award
for what he had not got through,

or where he had never been, or when,
how he could not grow up, (not why—),
but only the fact no one could live
under that shot-filled sky.

They had taken my children, as well, away,
and I had no choice except to serve,
to eat, to stay alive, and pray.
I was a pattern for their grave.

Weeping for her lost children, I,
Rachel upon the plains of salt,
of stone, of ivy. We had grown
like so much misbegotten clay,

for God or the State, too many. They
wisely decided that some must go
in order that the rest might stay
and pulled their numbers from a sieve
in a mock lottery to see
who'd chance to be or not to be.
Sieves hold no blood; the blood leaks through.

"I'm sorry, son, you're twenty-two."
"My number's up," he used to say.
His mother put his clothes away.
Above his grave some grass looks up

to all the unresponsive skies
that man has seen before or since
where no one keeps the dark accounts
he pays in guilt or innocence.

HE IS INDUCTED

I have given away my toys,
my tennis rackets and books,
to resign to the great song of time
the brief syllable of my life.

The days of amusement are gone
and the sorrowful instant come
when memory turns around
to look at the things that will be
and forget the passions that were.

And what then has grown in my mind
to reject the sweet bliss of earth
that is born and then it is gone?
No one will tell you this.

The sun in a circle goes;
the moon in a wink is down;
the leaves close and then unclose;
O what is found or not found?
What, then, shall I dream or choose
now all defenses are down
when I hear the last bells sound?

THE YOUNG RECRUIT

I cannot recall, except with tears,
this murderous lie. They call it war,
the time that takes, with many tears,
this boy uncertain of his crime,
    (They call him theirs)

and bows his head, who has no years
to pay life for, not knowing love,
nor having lived, or ever lay there
in the white clear field of the dove,
    (Oh, him they'll have!)

or the dove's vision. No recall
is his to mask his memory's sweep
or his heart's clock, which counts the hours
between him and his girl asleep.
    (But him, they'll keep.)

How is it that youth, ripest of all,
most beautiful, for his mother, when she is praying,
to hold nearby, where her hand, like a shawl,
still shelters one whose experience is too small,
is yet more ripe for slaying?

Indeed he is, in many ways, a child.
And I, whom many years have made less wise,
who have less reason in this difficult matter;
who never was in a war, or near a field
in which dead bodies lay in a giant scatter,
they do not want at all.

How often did I see them crowned with roses
or from the dim sea's dream come whistling down
that now the great red eye of war discloses
to be more futile than a blind man's clown.
    ("Man proposes—")

9

For what blind purposes? As "man proposes,"
(or once they said), as surely "God disposes."
Would one so young be useful? If let grow,
his mind, in future years become more fertile,
        (or I think so,)

perhaps would find some remedy for war.
Christ, what are armies for? They do not build;
I never found a battlefield yield more
of gold, or glory, tarnished as it were.
(O, what is glory for?)—

here where the blood lies still
and will not answer youth's last feverish cry
or climb again spring's bright and sun-blessed hill,
here, near the sky—
O, why?

That flower-crowned head, the sea-bedewed hair;
those eyes so bright with laughing! O, lie there,
too young to know what death is! Turn your head,
O, do not look! There are always too many dead—
O, how near!

AUTUMN, WAR

I sit here somewhere between October and November
in the sun, next to the ammo, watching the
    trucks go by,
in my own broken truck, wating to be rescued,
and the sights of war offend my appalled eye.

Somewhere out there is the North out of which
    winds come
and Winter, and the Devil, and glaciers;
North is full of caverns and raving monsters
far too fearful to deny.
North is where Hanoi is, Siberia, Moscow,
Korea, the Great Wall of China, Manchuria, Tibet,
inescapable mountains dissecting the frightful air.
Christ! Do not send us there!

THERE WAS WAR ON THE SLOPES OF THE MOUNTAINS

There was war on the slopes of the mountains,
the peaceful valleys where the dovecots were,
where the vines grew, and barrels overfull
of wine, and honey in the hive;
the blood rolled down the mountains and they fled;
the people fled; the small birds flew away;
the houses were deserted, and the streets
where bloody arrows flew; the cisterns filled
with blood, and in the darkened sky,
where the snow was, that held the veils of light,
a red glow rose, and bloody was the night
in the day of the tiger, the day of the wolf.
Man ranged against man, an earthly judgement.
Strike down the dawn, and cancel all the fires,
those, heaven's hurtless fires in the sky,
that gentled all the crops, and made them grow—
with an entire fall, they were no more.

THE THIN RED LINE

What am I doing here, at the turn of morning,
when the darkness falls to nature, watching men fight?
Here, in eternal loneliness, and mourning
for families lost, still watching this death's strife?
Have I nothing better to do? Are there not stars
out there, where the woods remain, so cold and deep?
Is there not sleep, that cure for every horror?
Or shall it bring the many dreams I keep
where my dead father visits, or those brothers
I never can forget? Eyes that tears wet
for the strange tricks the mind plays, when no home
exists for us, the banished, we who roam;
and when no love ever comes to trouble our lives
with doubts and prayers, nor even joy, that breath,
will bring such dreams of loves that never come
to such as are not loved—nor shall be yet.
O mockery of the air! when the moon sets,
that cold ironic grave of unreal light,
then on the earth a shadow rises. Here, O here,
is the unalterable moment of true sight.

FAR OTHER ARMIES, OTHER WARS

These ruins stand that once were Greece;
there is the cradle, here the lathe,
and underneath the bridge are laid
the young centurions in their brave
and ruinous armor. It is said
that dead men have no tears. I shed
their tears for them.
And many others, being as afraid,
have thought how the same love
moves through the race of man,
have thought of Hector silent in his tent,
Achilles wild in grief upon the plain
and how cold winds will weave their dusts about
that no descendants honor; how that vain
and splendid love that turns all those who live
whispers that wisdom lies not with the wise,
for all of wisdom is but half of love.

TO MY COUNTRY; TO MY GOD
(In Vietnam)   (What the son said.)

You will kill me; you will kill me,
    and shall I praise you for that?
Out of my prison praise that profane hand
that nourished me, when I, an ignorant fool,
was born, and had done nothing?...brought on me
your guilt, and in the long years' debacles
still tortured me with this unpitied will
too full of evil to be evil of itself,
but it must be infused with it to dwell
in such inspired anger and despair
that never end, but go from crime to crime
in mounting passion? Shall I live in this,
and live in hell before hell comes? And still
throughout it all sing praises of that joy
nevermore mine to see, that does not live,
and I doubt ever shall? I'll be your child—
your hating child, and, flouting all your power,
count me already damned, as sure I was
being first born, then kept alive, in this,
your infamous, and your, your pitiless world.

When did we ever learn, that we did not weep,
or weep, that we did not so for inestimable pain;
when did we ever know, but when knowledge wore
the cloak of habitual grief? When ever gain
any but partial wisdom; permanent woe?
What, shall I stand and watch, and watch and die?
Or worship where I'm paralysed with grief
and grimed with desperation and despair
to see so many fall? Shall I watch babes,
all whom the fire frights, and the heat sears,
and still do nothing, nothing? Have I a heart
to feel, a will to act, senses to weep,
and shall do nothing?
Am I a machine, or some abstracted saint
who prays in some soft darkness, never seeing
what God does all about him? Am I that,
and have not eyes to see, heart to have tears,
or breath to shed them with?

13

MORNING AT THE FRONT

The world is dark and far.
The birds lie early still.
And all about us are
the workings of His will.

Always the same great star
crosses the wandering sky;
over and over fly
the rapid whippoorwill,

seeking what is to tell;
wrapped in what other sky.
How deep the dark clouds lie
crowded against the hill!

Mist rises under grass;
the little mice lie still.
Time, like an angry glass,
flashes a faint thin chill.

The birds flock down the hill;
the little fawns run by;
the white clouds now lie still
locked in the lake's dark eye.

Summer is gone, and I
run with the first bright dew
into the spinning sky
as all slain soldiers do.

UNDER FIRE

I cannot learn it anymore—
all the magnificent mind of man
had once to say, or twice to say.

Down the bombs pour—
thousands of them, the seeds of sound,
gardens of doom, with weeds well thronged:
the dead, the nearly dying, leaves.

I, too, am dying, like the sound
a music makes, that's drawn away
till one can't hear it anymore;
know where it went: will it still play?
I, too, endure the banishment
of weary day from weary day.

Night intercepts between, of course,
but no one tells how long its stay:
why such things come, or go away.

Who is it that comes? Or man
or perfect beast? Human,
if that is human that may be
torn apart; his two halves torn
from the dark birth to the dark tomb.

THE DRAFT BOARD

Here is where the young man comes
to be crucified, as Christ stood
before the board of Pilate with His life.
(Unto the hands of the State I commend my soul;
the neighboring bullets and the warm, unfriendly
    breath
of the cannons.) Here they come,
eighteen and unprepared, childish, sweet,
afraid and innocent. O you who wait
at the hill's brink for ageless death's cold
    quiver
to fill or sink,
think, in your fever,
how once a young girl laughed and dipped in ink
the pen that signed your life away forever.

THE WOUND

Here in this burning end-land where
the heat makes dead leaves writhe across our hearts;
where springtime never starts,
but only clouds....
let the moon come lower and lower
that all the ground must cover
in one more lonely room,
shut out from life, life's sun;
life's sun of joy and tears,
isolated, spent,
alone, aloof,
I look within myself.....
I emptied long before
the storehouse of the mind.
Nothing is left there, or
the shades of nothing wait
to lead me where
night and day go straight
into a single grey,
unmarked. I say,
"What shall become of the Lord's prisoner
when he has no more sight, nor world to see?"
And I would bow my knee, but have no knee,
no, hand, no lip, no thought; no, I am all
I was before: a shadow. And the wall
the shadow falls on, fades. There is no wall;
the shadow falls and falls. There is no end to falling
when all the walls are down. Across the universe
the shadow falls; it falls forever turning
between the dead stars and the murdering day.

THE WOUNDED SOLDIER

"I do not wish to die, nor wish to live,
nor any other wish that falls to man.
And yet I will not stay, no, not stay here,
here in this world that reeks of all I hate:
this graveyard of dead souls. What choice is ours
when all the gates are shut, and the locks drawn?
What choice in this but age, but an old age
that has no blessing in it? No, I'd rather go
with youth still near me, hope still scattered high;
it's not the dying after that I fear,
it's life too long drawn out, till it becomes
a moldy thread: a history of dead days;
a story with no ending. It is here
the climax is; it's here I feel the fire
of life when it burns highest—then it explodes,
goes flying over the universe, as when at night
the splendid rockets open pleats of fire,
and blossom high in darkness like a spilled
and opened dawning that in one small hand
holds morning, like a star.

      This is my morning: here is my new dawn;
here my beginning that but seems an end.
O, do not weep, you spirits, that so long
have waited out the range of earthly days
now come to heavenly. Do not weep again;
O, do not fall, you trees, you earthly gates,
nor all these walls of wind, and walls of light,
that seem to close me, that, invisible,
can scarce veil what they hold.
No, do not weep, my pale inarticulate ghost,
that owns no words to tell me what you fear:
there's heaven in the morning.
        If I go,
I go not weeping; go not pale to go;
not fearful; not reluctant; not afraid,
but eager, to the arms of that which is
my soul's sweet memory."

THE WOUNDED SOLDIER DREAMS OF PEACE

Peace and beauty are the same;
where they move great circles are;
all the worlds move in this way.
Far above, the splendid wheels
of the universe obey.

   I, who watch, stand from this day
in awe of this magnificence,
that I cannot come or stay,
but mutely watch while far above
unknown worlds put on display.

And I am challenged by heaven for this:
Can I, the smallest, not obey?
Is all peace there, and none for me?

In the white moonlight I have lain
and dreamed dark dreams, while far above
the unperturbed planets lay;
the undisturbed stars went on—
they do not dream; not they.

In the white moonlight I have lain
under endless seas above,
blue and blue as far above
as the endless centuries move,

and dreamed and dreamed the eternal dream
man in his innocence puts on,
while high up in the heavens stream
laws he can neither know nor love.

THE BLIND SOLDIER

By sight we're neither known nor know:
and though the fields were freshly green;
the moon as white as rose in snow
or sunset's long slant slumber-beam
that round the world's swift turnings go
till everywhere there is a dawn;
though on the waves white sea-birds show,
and all the sky's one dazzling bow,
I shall not mourn for what I've seen,
that cannot see it anymore,
but bless the splendid and wise ghost
whose beauty needs not eye or ear
but is so shatteringly near
I cannot lose it or be lost.

VIETNAM

Rain, do not fall
on the young men who lie
in the dark and the wet
under the great
grey gloom of the sky
in a land far away
in a Vietnamese war.

Rain, do not pour
on these faces and hands
so cold that lie there
under the far
implacable fire of an
unseeing star.

Wind, do not run
with soft-fingered sands
across and across
those desolate lands
seeking to wake
the sweet myth of breath,
or love, which once filled these hands,
all spilled by death.

THE WASTELAND

Infinite squalor; war
the unspeakable squalor of a death-like prison.
O, not so far!
Here, where the never-risen,
lost in the murky clouds that bear no vision
wander so naked there;
here where the unread book, the undreamable word
fade with the century's smoke
into something indefinable, absurd:
the terrible terrain
filled up with rain;
crevice and nook
holding in unequal strain
a world damned with a look
to unutterable, final ruin.
Raincloud and plain
slumped down, where shook
the implacable Cain
his fist; where murder took
its first stalk in the world
and all the clouds unfurled
their reddened undersides.
Let the worm rise
that eats men's brains.
Throw down all the dreams,
the long-sought remains
of animal and fish
gone down like drains
where nature has its wish
that all things must go.
Under the hollow
and inside the cairne
the cryptic bones lie—
God's architecture
in a twisted lie.

"Ruin!" cry, cry!
The lost cities gone.
The animals die.
The bombs on and on.
Man, like a mad
irresponsible clown
left in command
of desert, and dry,
rainless forever,
bright empty sky
where the birds were
and the long quiet sea
with all its fish drowned,
belly-up in the sun
on the terrible shore—
O, ruinous man,
inheritor of
the bright shining galaxy
and a world full of broken glass,
beer cans, and rodents.

When no oil wells flow
and all the pretty trees
finally cut down,
never to grow,
    then drink the terrible brine.
    Be quiet, mind.

A SOLDIER WEEPS OVER THE ACCIDENTS OF WAR

But is this life's reward to be denied
the things that honor makes and fame keeps good?
To see my happiness has been destroyed
that used to sit above me as a god?
But is this joy to lie here without hope,
waiting for anguish, that pours down like rain;
to sift out pain, that measures its full scope;
to count old wounds, that part and open again?
O is it peace to look upon the past
and see dear friends lie there beneath the wheel
that crushed them, whom we sent there at the last,
remembered all too late, too far to heal?
How far away the dead are! We who live
have all the room of the world in which to grieve.

HE MOURNS FOR HIS BROTHERS

We must endure the rain and passing days,
the nights that rattle and refuse to stop.
No one has asked for this, nor given praise
for such unfitted slumber and false crop
that waits through countless winters for one spring,
wearing life's years as one would wear a shroud
knotted in dungeons by some dirgeful king,
as the forgetting blood would cry aloud,
forced to return, not knowing how to sing,
an empty fancy and a sorcerer's dream,
and yet more real than life, as truth would ring
out truth, and bring the lie, and that would seem
as the two halves of the world were meant to grow
into an inward and an outward woe.

THE BALLAD OF THE CHILD

PART I

The winter sun had just begun
His sharp peaks to decline
And in the blue cup of the sky
To pour a darker wine,

When at the ridge I saw a bridge;
The river curdled under.
Along the rail there stood a crowd
In silence and in wonder.

They told me that a child was lost
Where waters never waken.
As from a grave they tried to save
What was already taken.

I went down through the frozen fields—
From every stalk of wheat
The winter-flowers of the snow
Shook flowers at my feet.

I saw an icy river-bank,
A rowboat, and great trees;
Yet *all* there was I had not seen:
For more was there than these:

The air was singing; winter pulled
Its many strings of frost,
Where, as upon a harp, the wind
Its great bow crossed and crossed.

And now the sun, like a great gong
Was sounding in the sky—
The sun was still, and in the chill
I heard the moon pass by.

The moon passed by beneath the sun,
And still she mounted higher;
For on the whetstone of the sun
The granite moon struck fire!

A great wind rose: a soundless wind—
Deep as the hush of night,
And in the middle of the moon
I saw a fearsome sight—

A black spot grew; it changed and grew,
It was nor shallow nor deep,
But on her face, in stainless grace,
It moved as if in sleep.

All Nature changed; my blind-flesh flared,
And through me, thrill on thrill,
I felt the rush of the great wings
That are so beautiful.

Blue as a plum's breath was the sky;
The Earth was white beneath.
And every branch and grass stem bore
The mark of winter's teeth.

Each stalk did show white plumes of snow,
And it was very cold,
Yet that hard Earth, and that hard sky,
Held all that June can hold!

I felt the murmuring of flowers,
The hum of summer bees,
And through the veil of snow's white sail
I saw the green of trees!

Did summer with her troops and state
And spring with all her laces
Come only to my mind to show
The needlessness of places?

It did not matter where we were,
Nor matter spring or fall;
We are as undefined as those
Who come to no one's call;

We are as undefined as winds
Or what the winds are blowing,
And we may have as bright a cause,
And have as far a going.

PART II

The people stood about the wood—
Not one of them did falter;
They were as ones who wait the God
At a strange and unseen altar.

They were as ones who wait the God,
And now I felt Him coming!
The whole Earth moved while I stood still;
My blood moved to His drumming!

A sigh went round; the child was found—
A stir was on the place;
Then in the water and the ice
We saw a tiny face:

I felt for him a rush of love
That I had never known—
To seize him in my arms and kiss
Those lips so like my own—

To seize him in my arms and break
The seals that were upon him—
To open like a flask and shake
My own life-thirst upon him.

My heart was pounding and I shook
Like love's own ravished maiden:
Or was it death, or was it love,
With which that boat was laden?

Or was it love, or was it death,
That caused me so to shiver?
The cold of Time is a long, long cold
More deep than any river;
The cold of Time is a true, true cold
Which Death comes to deliver—

Now barbarous in ancient gold,
A Pirate at his treasure,
In masked array he took his prey:
We watched him at his pleasure!

Death grew pale as if he'd ail;
A fever was upon him.
He drank his venom and we found
The mark of Time upon him!

PART III

Ah, seven is a perilous age
That has nor fear nor sense.
He all alone met the unknown
And offered no defense:

28

Why was he here, and all alone,
On ice that would be splitting,
To open like a shears and cut
The thread his life was knitting?

The Earth betrayed him in his trust,
And cruelly she did shatter
The dream, the beauty, that he was,
As if it did not matter!

The man bent down, and to the boat
He drew the child around;
He clutched him tight in both his arms
As if he too would drown!

The little child, so pitiful,
So pale and wan he lay
His tiny arms outspread to reach
So blindly for the day!

His hands were open, and his lips,
Those little sieves in water,
Let fall each drop, as if to stop
The channels of all slaughter—

The water's weight had closed his eyes,
He looked as he were sleeping,
Save for the cold immunity
He showed to pain or weeping:—

Indifferent as the arch above,
And in as cold a slumber;
The Earth could move him with her love,
Or move him with her number,
But he would lift no little hand
To lightning or to thunder;
No, he would lift no little hand
Though Earth itself went under!

In perfect disobedience
To any human laws,
He kept the kingdom of himself
And sought no other cause—

And though his mother called his name,
And broke her heart with aching,
He had forgotten any claim
Save those his dreams were making.

> *There was a radiance in the sky*
> *Not made by any weather;*
> *The people felt it in their blood*
> *And crowded close together.*

> *The people felt it in their blood;*
> *It joyously did shower,*
> *And everyone that stopped that day*
> *Felt a sure and awful power—*

> *They knew it certain as the knife*
> *That cuts the birth-cord's tether:*
> *The bright and turning knife of death*
> *That joins new cords together.*

PART IV

The sun was singing in the sky:
The whole Earth seemed to sing;
The child was snuggled in the vast
Warm comfort of God's wing.

We climbed with him across the hill
And through the snowy field,
And all the way we tried to stay
The clay that he would yield.

As in the shadow of the sun—
Of his own light the breaker!
He shone, and at his feet there stood
The armies of his Maker.

I looked about and saw the crowd,
And, O my heart was driven!
My little girl was wreathed in smiles!
I saw the smiles of Heaven!

Yes, everyone, each face, I'm bound,
In shame and glory, smiled—
And then their eyes they all cast down,
Bewildered as a child!

I saw the bright probe of the sun,
The arrows in his quiver;
And where they struck there rose a ray
Of fire from the river

The many diamonds of the snow
Held light that doubled vision,
And where it lay was a strange play
Of phosphorescence risen:
And all the ice, as in a vise,
Held rainbows in a prison!

PART V

Now death, who comes in double guise,
Had gone and left us shaken:
But we had seen, if we were wise,
 If he had given or taken!

For that dark angel made of wings,
 And made of light and thunder,
Brought to our minds strange echoings
From a far land of wonder.

He wears the veil through which no spark
Is caught or ever seen;
Yet though his evenings may be dark
His dawns are bright and clean.

We had a sip as from the lip
Of Life that is not wasted,
And it had left us drunk and wild
With wine we'd never tasted.

The ancient sun now in the sky
In all his stars assembled;
Beneath this hood of fire stood I
And looked on it, and trembled:

The leaf was broken from the stem;
The bell-string from the zither—
Yet this small child, from self exiled,
Would grow and never wither!

EPILOGUE

Although no mortal can resolve
The ways of God to man,
I know this much; it falls to us
To make them what we can;

For each thing lost at such dear cost
We'll give the world another!
And if it asks us we will pay
A brother for a brother.

So for the little child it took
In beauty and in sorrow,
I give the world this little book—
Keep it for tomorrow.

THE DEATH OF THE SOLDIER

"What do I see! Those pinwheels in the sky!
More clear, more bright than ever stood before
the unread augurs of the sun and moon,
the fiercely colored comet that returns....

Ah! It draws me up; it draws me up again!
I will not live! Oh, damn you for a fool!
I only meant to struggle, not to die!
       Ah, now I feel it burning—ah, my brain!
The image of my thoughts is all turned round.
I'll have no more conceiving: none at all!
No towering instants when I thought to draw
the ends of being in a knot, a dream—
as men do dream, being in their ecstasy,
some ancient god, some very ancient god.
No more tomorrows when the bright sun was
the rival of my bright imaginings;
no more love moments when the glittering hours
were scattered by the sweet pain of a kiss
when love had made a heaven to be lost....
perhaps I'll find it now?
       Oh, let me go!
I've used up all my tears; they burn; they burn!
You cowards, who have taken me from the world
when it and I most loved. May world!
May evening filled with mists ...
... and morning, that will come ... or will it come?
Now is dark indeed—
but yet more dark approaches!
       Oh, to dream
would be a mighty gift.
       Do the dead dream?"
          (he dies.)

THE BALLAD OF THE DEAD SOLDIER
The Wife's Lament

Now he has gone so far, so far,
who used to lie so close,
and all I see is a white, white sheet
that's like a living ghost.

O wide and wide is the counterpane
and nothing lies between
and from my arms is all I've had
and from my heart the same.

For in my arms he slept last night;
all night the birds would cry.
"So nature stirs them in their hearts,
they have to sing," said I.

"God loves the world so much," I said,
and whispered close and small—
O God, now where is lain your head?
And where your living soul?

The room is empty, open, wide;
the halls are empty, too,
and nothing comes between us both
but a cold wind creeps through.

And nothing in the great dark comes:
no light, nor yet no star,
but only the small singing bird
who sang to us before.

I learned the song from lips now still
that once could sing so high—
the night-bird sings of joy until
he breaks me with his cry.

THE RETURNED VETERAN REMEMBERS HIS COMRADES

Why should I care; why should I love,
when those I loved most, passed away,
first from the world, then from my hands;
my eager breath, that begged them, "Stay!"
There, where my eyes could never see,
nor my voice call, nor hear at all—
nor my arms hold, though I had held
myself apart, and wished them here,
keeping a place, a heart, a bed,
through summer's long declining year
and winter's clouds that still lie spread
across the dawns and sunsets there
making the sky one funeral red.

"They may return," O, it was said;
"They may return," but was not meant,
and long has it been promised,
like heaven, or the spring's return,
or hope, or harvest to the dead.

THE DREAM OF THE SOLDIER

I was in hell, but, O, I was half free!
I called out to another if by chance
he also lived in this dark circumstance
of inward fires that no one else could see.
But he turned back from me.

I bear a corrupt vision in a brain
no angel ever visits—no soft touch
will come and bid my dreadful thoughts to hush
and loneliness is with me once again.

I tire of the treadmill of these dreams
that nightly stalk me with their endless strain
telling me nothing over and over again:
telling me all that seems, or seems to pass,
is but reflection, and a shattered glass.

HIS BRIDE WELCOMES THE RETURNING SERVICEMAN

The worlds are made of wind and rain;
Full of white splendor is the sea.
The birds are singing once again.
O rise, my love, and come to me.

Not of the things of now and then,
Those that the world accounted fair,
Now that sweet summer's come again
Shall we be mindful, or shall care.

Full of white shadows is the sun;
The silver lake, the winds, obey.
Out of their mists the bright clouds run;
Out of their nests the small birds stray.

When you shall see them you shall come,
Ah, but my heart shall run to hear!
Ah, but I hear his footstep home,
Ah, but my blood tells me he's near.

Swifter than swallows is my love,
Swift as the sun when light appears,
When in an instant all is done
And the dark planet slowly clears.

Closer than shadows is my love,
Bright as bright shapes the moon may wear
When she is deep, and the clouds run
Under her shadow, far and near.

Sweeter than summer is my love,
Sweeter than apple or round pear
When the rich boughs are overborne
With the ripe cherries waiting there.

Brighter than summer is my love,
Than the bright world, O, far more fair!
Bright as two stars, when first they move,
Than all their beauty when they're near,
A heaven, and a blazing air!

36

THE DEATH OF THE SUBMARINE

Dedicated to: The Men of the Thresher and the Scorpion

I. Introit
The Sea

Though it is very strong;
though it is very deep,
the sea can never keep
fire for long;

out of the climbing wave,
out of the seal's tusk,
it took what these men gave:
only a husk.

Death is a pair of shears,
a vast divider;
that which remains appears
to the outsider

but to her inward grace
no man has motion:
those who would see her face,
seek first the ocean.

All things that die in her
die to their doubt.
Though you are doubly lost
she finds you out.

Pearl and the seed of pearl!
Light and the seed of light!
That which we tightly furl
shall be set loose tonight!

II. The Submerging

The sea has bubbles undersea
that move her in her power
as in our blood the bubbles globed
and burst, in our last hour.

Above us the waves and sun
make ceaseless quarrel upon the points of light,
but where we are is night
forever starless. Moonless, underneath the sea,
no worlds are born. No twilights mark
the boundries of our gateless dark—
night unremitting; night no moon may bless—
the sultan, night, in his mysterious dress.

The emerald shifting draperies of the sea
parted for us. For us
the drawbridge slowly rose; the stately locks
were broken, every one. For us
the gates of earth were lifted. Now there was
only great peace, and more than peace: now free,
the burden of the body was no more.

I spilled the sorry wine; I broke the crust;
I fed on food that had been held from me.
I drank the milk of angels — now each drop
of ocean's rangeless waters ranged in me
and I became as mighty as the sea!

And in the coiled enchantment of her dream
her heart lay still ...
Like fireflies upon a summer's eve
Light wrinkled in the hollows of the waves,
or, like the stars that gem the Milky Way,
flashed, and was still.

Deep are the drafts of the silence we drink.
Slow are the drifts of the tides.
Soft is the night that her water contains—
Smooth are the veins of her, musical, musical.

There are bells in the sea; I hear them toll:
each wave is a bell, prolonged, resounding.
I am deep in the echoing choir of the sea.
She is my mother, singing to me.

III. The Death

I did not feel the heavy weight of time;
I did not feel the sea — I knew no more of pain
than does the child still nestled in the womb,
for death had made another child of me!

Above, the world was stormy; the rain
rang like a bell; it summoned me—
deep-throated, full-voiced, sonorous and resounding sea!
Sea mother! Sea twice-blessed!
I bless you in my birth and in my dying ...
I spend my blood upon you as one pays
an old and honorable debt: I give to you
no less than what you gave.

More than pearl is in the sea.
More than white bone the flesh receives.
For in the flesh, and of the bone
the spirit makes it breviaries.

Slowly we fell; we sank down, down,
into an ever deeper silence; a glaring dark,
tumbling through time and the sea, end over end,
and where we fell
in a great avalanche of steel
the sides of the sea
came together.

IV. The Awakening

When we look through the water at the moon
we see her magnified; her attendant stars
swim beside her, swollen with her fires—

This ship will never go
where the star-ships go,
shaped like them, to glide
through earth's vast pools and wide —
in heaven there is no hiding:
there all the stars are shown
vast in their splendor. Roll in fire,
O universe all fire!
Only here, in this pearl, this orient world,
have we caught in our hands the little fish
of eternity — the elusive silver fish
that breeds itself forever!

All down the long echoing corridors of the sea,
there where the kelp lies deep,
call us, call us, — but we
will never answer, being as we are
part of the core, the center of the sea.

Though my heart is cold, cold,
beyond the deepest cold
is a well of springing warmth
where the great hands unfold:

Nature rescues those she strands—
on the webbed white sea sands
mermaids hold me in their hands:
angels sing to me.

And time has bound his jewels about my head!
I am crowned with rings of light.
The emperor ocean keeps his court for me,
and many fishes, with their little lamps,
like candles in a crypt, dance in a ring
and make a gleaming festival of this,
our first contact with death.

AFTER THE WAR

I.

I must praise the world and all that's in it;
praise for the lute of the soaring linnet;
praise as the sunlight roars in the tree;
praise for the heat that burns upon me —
praise upon praise, until every minute
moves with a music in it.

I must praise with death all but upon me
and praise with the pain that locks my breath,
and praise with the lips with the dust
    upon them —
the dust that is my death:

World, I have loved you well!
World, you are hard to lose!
I am netted, consumed in your spell,
and it is as I choose.

Earth, you, not I, must die,
and in your radiant shroud
rain, for a thousand years
your life's aborted cloud.

The protons God had set in place
to hold the stately wheels of Space;
the atoms, in their ordained grace;
the order that arranged so well
the starry citadel —

The studded atoms that were firm,
those nails that held the sun and moon
and stars unborn, and all in tune,
each thing ordained to its due term:

42

All these, all these, we have destroyed;
the choirs of heaven, the vespers, stilled;
made sterile all the starry void
by the blood that we have spilled.

Then, then did we check the stars in
    their courses —
then did we cut the reins of the night,
and we have caught the moon
in a noose of her own light!

II.

Dark are the veins of twilight
that climb the sullied sky
in the doldrums of the sun
when the dawn has been put by
for our own false dawn, the shaking
of the flares of death-fires breaking.

O sorry world, that bears in such dark need
the endless silent millions of your seed;
and I, one who has loved you overmuch,
cry for the last bright blessing of your
    touch:

I crave your little leaves, that turned
upon the wind, and made the tree all white;
how soft the underpetals were, and sweet,
how sweet, the honeysuckle, the wild vines
that pierced me with the sharp blade of
    their beauty ...

And how the Springtime sang!
It mewed and purred, and in the glistening
    snow,
before the last breath of the frost,
in rapture opened reckless little petals,
and the daffodils, the crocus, would parade
flags upon winter's grave.

And I remember light ... the way it gave
shadows and sparkles on the hollow snow
or lay in calm serenity beneath
the willow's cloudy wreath ...

and I remember peace—the way it fell
to look upon the morning and know well
how surely evening comes; how sure the moon,
and each tomorrow with its afternoon.

How I remember peace! Who know no more,
after the world's destruction, after war,
but a long wandering, and a long despair:
and all about me nothing, nothing, nothing —
nothing there.

I shall eat of the poison fish
in that wasteland that was the sea,
and swept with its own perfume
its vast, uncurtained room;

I shall walk in the barren weeds,
and eat of the bitter herbs,
and drink of the little streams,
for the fruit is bruised on the vine.

And the clouds shall pour their poison rain,
and nothing green shall grow again
in the wasteland of the world.

But in my disembodied heart
I shall walk sheltered and apart.
The wind sings through me, dart by dart,
a many-colored harp, whose strings
are barren branches, broken wings,
and other disassembled things.

III.

The moon, like a white civet, wails,
beridden of the snow, and pales;
low on the white horizon lies,
shivers, and dies ...

and all is dead; the fields, the crimson grain;
the seed is dead; the seed that fell like rain
all the long summer on the thirsty plain
:hat shines now, like a mirror, in the sun—
the sand all glass! For now, in all this
    mirrored sphere
there is no one.

No one to see the crystal rocks that turn
light upon light until the eyelids burn.
No one to see the dazzle and the flash
of a world of ash.

No one to feel the cinders underfoot
or wipe away the soot
from all these tear-streaked faces.
No one to dig the graves; no one to plant
one single blade of grass; no one to look
for one last unburned book.

No one to make the shattered marble white,
scarred by the fallen flail of night,
or clean the broken cities of their rust,
or sweep the sterile dust.

No one to hear the silence; none to fall
beside me on these sands, this burning pall,
and weep with me for all that is undone.
No one to hear the hissing of the sun.

And nothing was as beautiful before
as this great sun, above this sunken sea,
caught in a net, reflected by the score
of all the mirrored false suns in the sky
that the glass Earth still flashes out and
    blends
until I cannot tell where light begins or ends,
or count the shattered rainbows in the sky;
and all the world is diamond, grimly gleaming;
cold, lifeless, and alone.

      Come, take this broken stone.
      Try now to till this soil.
      The hoe will bend and break
      on earth no toil can wake.

IV.

Sidereal spin and twist —
A comet is of amethyst.
The sapphires of the morning
are the blue-edged world-stars that hover
along the edges of the sky
where the shadows turn over and over
in death's last tryst.

For the night throws a thousand shadows,
and everywhere I can see
reflected in blank walls and chasms
the moon's dead mimicry.

For we have killed the Springtime; killed
    the leaves,
the dainty pearls of summer; killed the dawn ...
even the butterfly, his wings aflame,
has perished, and the birds choke on their
    song:

for we have made a winter overlong;
an endless darkness, in the lethal glow
of our last monument, the unmarked snow:

    Not a footstep mars my flame;
    not a whisper, not a name,
    and my white sepulchres shall be
    as empty as the cratered sea.

    As if one pinionned by a God
    I struggled; in the clotted sod
    I crawled, and then I reached the breach —
    Blinded, I fell upon the beach.

No more the sunset and the dawn!
No more to watch the cloud-wracked sphere
in the turning of the year ...
No more to see the crimson sun
with all its ribboned clouds undone
on that red hill, the last I saw
on the last day of the world.
Or hold night's funeral in fires—
obsequies of stars! For on their pyres
we burn our own eclipse.

I cannot see the shining blade
that cuts me down; but now a stark
and sudden lightning; then the dark.

INDEX OF FIRST LINES

INDEX OF TITLES